GOD'S AMAZING HANDS

CYNTHIA PHILLIPS

Printed in the United States of America.

ISBN
979-8-88945-146-4 (Paperback)
979-8-88945-147-1 (eBook)

Brilliant Books Literary
137 Forest Park Lane Thomasville
North Carolina 27360 USA

Original Painting by Cynthia Phillips

TABLE OF CONTENTS

Chapter

ONE

Nothings Ever Going to be the Same

Cynthia writes; nothing within me could prepare me for this day. I never wanted this day to come if possible. But all the wishing in the world was not going to change this.

It was Father's Day, June 12, 2003, and my youngest son Sean was going off to California to be a Marine. This has been his dream for many years. My husband and I on the other hand tried our best to change his mind. But that was not to be. Our oldest son Kyle was married, living nearby but he would come along with us to the recruiter's office with his wife, Virgie. We knew this would be the last we would see Sean for 12 weeks. Packed and ready to go Sean was excited as well as apprehensive. You could feel the anticipation as our son wondered what life would be like away from home and away from all he had ever known. There was sadness when Kyle left home to get married but happiness in knowing he would now be linked to a new addition-his wife. But with Sean leaving, I could only think of the possible dangers that could befall this vibrant young man. The Iraqi War was on and nothing was normal about this war. The TV was filled with the news about Iraq. It was heartbreaking to hear of the deaths of our boys and girls over there. And now our son was going over there.

We had our last breakfast with him at a waffle diner across the road from the Mall where the recruiter's office was located. The hour had come to send our son off to train as well as other family's sons with hugs, handshakes, pictures, and tears.

Before we knew it he was ready to leave with the others as they drove off, out of sight. I went into a deep, dark depression at this point. How am I going to handle this? What am I going to do?

We got back to the house and it felt like part of my heart was gone. I walked around like a zombie with an unknown destiny. With a part of my heart missing and no known help, I chose to mow the lawn. This was a riding mower and if I could get my mind off of this boy it would be a miracle I thought. Anything would be easier than sitting in the house that's for sure. So off I go, just me and the lawn mower with a half-broken heart. But as I rode on the mower, I began to cry. It was a culmination of all the hurt and pain plus the noise of the mower. What will happen to him, will he fight in this war, will he be killed, and will we ever have a normal life again? As this mowing went along something was at my right side staying with me everywhere I went! I looked to my right but I couldn't see a thing, but I knew she was there! It was Mema, my maternal Grandmother. She had been dead for 32 years! How could this be? Am I losing my mind? What is going on? I drove along quietly with her spirit staying right with me. If I sped up she sped up. If I slowed down she slowed down. It was so real I even talked to her for a moment or two. Mema, what is going on? How can you be here? Am I finally losing it? Every few minutes I would look to my right to see if I could see her but it wasn't to be. She had chosen to come to me when I needed her the most. The farther I got the better I felt, but she still stayed right next to me. Somehow she was telling me everything was going to be all right. There would be no death, he would come home safe. I had nothing to worry about! Wow, this is fantastic! My crying had stopped and I actually had a smile on my face. My heart knew I had received wisdom from above. This wisdom was eternal and beyond anything I had ever experienced. By the time the lawn was done she was gone but her presence had been felt, loved and appreciated at a most needed time.

Chapter

TWO

Mema My Rock

Ciny writes: It wasn't supposed to happen I said to myself. My Grandmother-Mema was not supposed to die, but despite my pleadings, the call came anyway. I was 18 years old and graduating from high school when the call came. I was only 8 years old when her daughter Mattie, my mother, died. My aunt Carrie Lou called to say Mema was in serious condition and that I needed to come soon if I wanted to see her alive.

The trip from Tulsa to Houston was a blur. A series of dreams the week before we left were going through my brain with a lot of confusion and denial. Three dreams one each night about Mema saying goodbye and dying. No, no, no, it can't happen she is so important to me she can't leave me alone. This was the Mema I loved so dearly. She was a large woman with a big stomach. It didn't matter to me though, her love felt like I could conquer the world. She was my rock, my foundation, my everything.

She took me into her home every summer and loved me as her own. We never missed church. That was so very important to her but you felt the love of God in that house. Her life centered on that big black book (the Bible) that she carried so diligently to church. Church was a part of my life when I stayed with her. I wanted to do what she said so off to church we went. It felt right in my heart.

We arrived at the Houston hospital much too quickly. She lay in her bed so small and petite I hardly recognized her. "Mema, I said, how are you?" "I'm not doing well", she replied.

We talked for a few minutes but she seemed distracted. "What is it?" I asked. "What is that strange box on the wall?" she pointed. "That is the TV Mema, so you can watch television."

"Oh," she said.

We didn't talk too much when all of a sudden she looked at me and said: "Mattie what are you doing here?" I was in shock, was she losing her senses? "No, Mema, it's me Cindy, Mattie's daughter." She shook her head no, and said "it's Mattie!" Over and over I said "no Mema its Cindy," but I could not convince her. I was sure she had lost it, medication, sickness, and such had made her lose her mental functions. No matter what I said she seemed to have her mind made up.

The look on her face was of a wonderful reunion, I decided not to argue anymore, she seemed so happy. The visit lasted for a short while and we were told it was time to leave. Over and over I kept playing the whole visit in my mind trying to make sense of a strange visit. We had a bite to eat and off to the Hotel we went for the night.

The next morning the phone call came that would change my life forever, Mema had passed away that very night, it was all so very sad and upsetting. The drive home was quiet with little conversation, but my thoughts kept returning to the visit. What did she mean by calling out my mother's name when she could see clearly that it was me standing there? What was that look of recollection and excitement? Years later I picked up a book about people seeing their loved ones who had passed from this life on to the next, and now I was in shock. Could this be what had happened to Mema and I, while I was standing in the way? It all seemed so strange yet somehow it felt right! My Mom must have come in the room while I was standing there and Mema could not get me to understand that she was not talking with me but was seeing into the spirit realm. Mom had come to take her Mother home to heaven and to see her daughter at the same time. Oh, how I wish I could have understood that day. I would have loved to hear what she saw and heard. How often do they come and check on us and we have no clue anything is any different? Since that day I believe I caught a glimpse of seeing a reflection of the afterlife and what it means to our passing relatives and friends. The comfort it must have given to Mema to know there is more to this life than what we can see or hear.

Chapter

THREE

Jail House Rocks

It was never easy to go there, the jail that is. For several years I had been making my way to the County jail on Wednesday nights. Some nights the pressure before going was overwhelming, to say the least.

There is a lot of evil spirits who belong to these men and women so praying before you go is very important. This night was going to be good, I told myself I prayed with everything I had within me and off I went.

Our jail was downtown and you go to the rear of the building and descend a ramp to a locked door and a buzzer. I buzzed as usual and the lock was opened. During this time you hear an alarm go off and you grab the door and pull. As I walk through the door the smell of this place is like a soggy basement because that is exactly what it is. As I go through the second set of doors I am greeted by the guard behind the window. She is always sitting there carefully watching cameras as they continually record all areas of the jail. After signing in I go past the men in two different cells and pass several prisoners who are trustees. Trustees are allowed to walk outside of the cells till bedtime.

The girls are always at the very end of the hall, there could be one cell full of them or two depending on how many they have to house. Robert was another person who always came on Wednesday nights too. I didn't see Robert that evening I could have just missed him or he could have been in another area, I only spoke with the women.

My routine was simple I would get down there and sit in my chair while I would do a Bible study with the girls who wanted to listen. I would conclude with a prayer in general or for their requests. After the study, I had a young lady who wanted to talk with me but this other girl kept talking and talking about mostly unimportant things almost as if to distract me from something. This other woman was distraught with something and I knew it.

Finally, I couldn't hold it any longer and told the one that kept talking I am sorry but I need to speak to this other woman would she mind talking to me later. Finally this woman came to the bars and proceeding in telling me her story. She explained that she had demons within her.

"Okay", I said and "why is that?" She told me her story of drugs and games that were not what she should have been doing and these demons had gotten her thrown in jail. I felt panic rush through me in a way I had never felt before. I yelled for Robert but they told me he was not here anymore. Fear rushed into me like a flood! There was not going to be any help, what was I thinking? I've never done this before! HELP what do I do? How do I do this?

Calmness came over me and I knew it was going to be me or nothing at all. I had prayed with others before that had demons but I always had the church people praying with me but not this time I was all alone. When I say I'm alone, I meant that I was the only physical person here. I was not alone the Lord was with me. Calmness within me rose above the fear. It was as if I was supposed to be here and supposed to do this. So I prayed in tongues over this woman as well as rebuking the demons to come out of, her. She shook and she cried and the sweat rolled over her in waves. It was very disturbing to see this; almost like a very personal thing happening and you are watching this unfold before you.

Then she collapsed. I explained to the girls they needed to care for her and to also give her space as she was still in a very fragile state. How did I know this, where is this wisdom coming from??? All the ladies seemed frightened, but I told them this was a good thing and that they had witnessed a woman being freed from these tormentors. Again, where is this coming from? But now I'm starting to get used to it. It felt comfortable and full of power. The whole time this was going on the ladies where lined up on the opposite wall. They knew what was happening but they were afraid of these spirits leaving her so they were as far away as they could get. I wish there had been more time. Time went by very fast now it was time for me to leave. As soon as the air hit my face the reality of what happened slammed into me. How could I have done this without any body to help me? What was I thinking, what did I do? I knew it was God and that the Lord had prepared me to be in the right place at the right time.

The next week I retuned she was waiting for me. She told me the demons were all gone and how did I do it? I didn't I told her it was the Lord who took them away. She had a smile on her face and she said she was free, free, and free! This woman was still locked up but she was freer than many people on the outside! That is when I told her not to get back with the same bunch of people she had been running with. She needed to get out and find a good church and go there on a regular basis. This was a turning point of her life. Hopefully she listened and started a new life with Christ as her partner. [Blank space was purposely done to follow traditional layout formatting standards]

Chapter

FOUR

Mission Impossible

As a hospital volunteer it was my job to pick up a list of patients from the Chaplains office and visit as many as possible before the day ran out or I ran out of energy. Walking on a cane took lots of strength to meet the normal obligations of the typical person. It was a fairly routine type of job. I would enter a room and say "Hello my name is Cindy from the Pastoral Care Department how are you?" This would bring either a good response back or if they were not interested in talking with me a grunt or a groan would come out" You could usually tell if" a person was interested in talking with you within the first two minutes. If a person was a talker any normal stay time in the room is around 10 to 15 minutes at most.

I was encouraged into Pastoral care at the age of 15 when I was hit by a boat and was paralyzed in the hospital. The nurses would dress me up, stick me in a wheelchair, and push me into a room. These people were either paralyzed very sick or extremely depressed. The nurses always told me if anyone can help them it's got to be you. Being so young I believed them so that was the beginning of my ministry"

On this one particular day, I was doing my rounds as usual with no indications of any differences at all. I always pray before I start my round as well as during which I am sure made the difference on this day. As I entered this room, there laid a man, I was going to say "Hello my name is Cindy form the Pastoral Care Department how are you?"

But that is not what came out of my mouth. "You know God loves you, don't you?" I could not believe it. What I had just said? That was not what I intended. The look on this man's face was shocked. His mouth flew open and he said nothing. But that is not what surprised me as much as I could not say a word after that. I was swept out of that room supernaturally! There was no way for me to move as fast as I did but it happened. I was in his room one minute and gone the next. As I stood outside his door it was as if something was blocking the way so I could not go back in! I was in shock, what just happened here? How did I not say what I intended to say? I haven't moved that fast since my running days! What is this energy blocking the door? It was an energy like I have never felt before or felt since. There was nothing normal about this, yet for some reason, I was involved.

Later on, I reflected on that incident and the only thing I can come up with was this. Maybe this man had talked to God before I got there and said to himself "I will believe in you, if the next person who comes into my room says, you know God loves you don't you?" I happened to be that person. God did a miracle for that man that day and me. One day when I get to heaven I will find out the whole story but till then I can only imagine. In the Bible God used a jackass to talk to a man, so why not me? Me being the jackass that is.

Chapter

FIVE

Cynthia Goes to the Fair

Cynthia writes: this was around 1980 and I was 28 years old. I was working at the Telephone Company at the time and I had a 1-year old. It was my day off from work and David and I were going to go to the races. The morning was busy with work at home cleaning and doing laundry as normal days went. David and I planned on him coming home from work and then we would take Kyle to his Aunt's and then we would go to the fair.

As I was cleaning in the living room I heard a loud audible voice saying' "Do not go to the fair." It scared the daylights out of me! I began to search the house thinking someone is here playing a trick on me but I found no one. Nothing like this had ever happened to me before, was I going crazy? Where did this voice come from? My mind was reeling with questions. What, how, why me? After several minutes of concern, I tried to get back to getting things done around the house" Well that was just the beginning: over and over and over this voice said the same words "Do not go to the fair, do not go to the fair, do not go to the fair." I felt like I was in some kind of a Sci-Fi movie. After some time I was beginning to think of ways to try and tell David I didn't want to go to the fair. It was obvious to my way of thinking that something was not right.

As usual, David got home at 4:30 pm and he was ready to go. I tried to talk him into going somewhere else but he could not be convinced. I was NOT going to tell him about the voice for fear of him thinking I was crazy. Boy, was that a mistake. We got to the fair just fine and it was misting rain the whole evening. For some stupid reason I still don't know why I thought if I kept my hair dry everything would be all right. Well, my hair was dry the whole time, what a relief I thought. Then it was time to leave. Thank goodness I thought the sooner the better. I couldn't shake that voice. David told me to wait at the ticket counter so he could get the truck and pick me up. I waited and waited and waited. The traffic was terrible, line and lines of cars trying to leave. Finally, I saw his truck waiting to get into traffic. It was just a short way over to him and then we could leave this crazy place because I still had an uneasy feeling about being here. So I walked across two lanes of traffic to David's truck. I stopped at the front driver's side and waved at him. I could have sworn he saw me, so I proceeded to walk over to my side of the truck. Before I could even realize what was happening he proceeded to drive forward! I fell and rolled up into a ball. It all happened in a kind of slow-motion movie. The left front tire rolled up onto my back and he stopped. Time just kind of slowed way down, I was looking at the rear tire knowing if he kept going forward or to the left he was going to run over my head. I started screaming at the top of my lungs with every breath I had. I don't think I have ever been as scared as I was at that moment.

Nothing was happening! The noises from the fair were drowning out my screams? And if that wasn't bad enough I couldn't seem to change the tone of my screams it was like all the screams going on at the fair? Oh my God, I am going to die today and it is going to be very painful when he runs over my head like a cantaloupe. Why didn't I listen? Who's going to raise my son? How bad is this going to hurt? If only I could change things! There was no pain while I lay there with the truck on my back, just fear at its worst. It couldn't have been more than a minute or two, but it felt like an eternity before I heard a man yell at David "Stop" he said you just ran over a lady.

David rolled down his window and said "you are kidding." I didn't run over anyone.

"Yes, you did", he said, she is right under your front left tire. After backing off of me he jumped out of the truck and was in shock to see it was me! I heard him say "oh, no it's my wife." The crowd was in shock. They thought he was trying to kill me, but I was not where I was supposed to be, waiting at the ticket counter. One lady said, "it will be okay once you get to the hospital." Another was patting my arm. Looking down at me on the pavement, with her face said this couldn't get any worse. They told me not to move the ambulance was on the way. As I lay there I realized my hair was soaked! Why hadn't I listened? How could I have done this to myself? This should have never happened. If I had told David about the voice this never would have happened. The ambulance ride was going to be the red lights and sirens all the way, they told me. After getting in, they did their procedures with accuracy and with complete confidence. This was good for me because distractions were what I needed the most. Distractions from keeping me from thinking about the truck hitting me, knocking me down on the asphalt, the truck stopping on my back, and everything else going along these lines. When out of the blue I thought to myself "I can't feel any pain." Having been paralyzed, this part of the ride was utter terror. The EMT assured me that it was normal for your body to go into a shock. It made sense and from that point till we got to the hospital was calmness and lots of questions in my heart. After getting to the Emergency Room things slowed down and tests were taken. It almost felt like they couldn't find anything wrong.

He would send me for a test and that test came back fine. Finally, the doctor said to me that he was going to let me go home! He couldn't find anything wrong with me. HELLO! I was just run over by a truck Doc! This has to be the strangest thing in my life! What can I say Doc? Turned out I didn't have too. This sweet, wonderful, smart nurse spoke up. Excuse me, Doctor, do you mind if I speak with the patient for a moment? I could sense the relief the Doctor felt at that moment was huge. Certainly, he breathed. With certain quietness and with respect she spoke to me. Cynthia, we are going to pick up your right side okay? Oh no, I said, it's going to hurt so badly. No, no, no, no..... ugggg. I know you have to. Yes, we have too. As she picked up the hip I screamed in pain, the Doctor jumping back a bit. He immediately said something to the effect of I think we have found the problem here. Off to X-ray, I went. Those X-rays showed and almost shattered right hip, with a bruised heart. With much relief, they finally admitted me and I had one special nurse to thank.

Right after arriving at the ER, the Police arrived. They pulled David to the side and asked me over and over what happened at the fair tonight? We don't believe your story about you being in an accident. So......... You want the truth? You want the truth, I said? Yes, two of them said with grins all over there face and pen and paper in hand. I will tell you the truth, so again I told them the story about the ticket counter and waiting to be picked up. It was like someone had pulled the plug out of them. The pen dropped to the side, the paper was being crushed in their hand. Are you sure this is the real story? Yes, I said, it was exactly as I told you. They didn't believe a word I said. They thought I was covering up a messed up possible homicide!

Sometime during this fiasco, my Dad showed up. I told him the story just as I had to the cops, the nurses, and the doctor. For some reason, I don't think he believed me either. He just kept saying to David "How come you didn't see her?" "what's wrong with you, why didn't you see her?" As he explained to the cops his defroster was not working and I was supposed to be waiting at the ticket counter and it was misting rain. His radio was on so he never heard the screams. None of this mattered to me. I wasn't supposed to be here, remember? I didn't listen. I never blamed David because it wasn't his fault. I didn't listen. Or should I say I didn't obey what I was told to do? This didn't help David of course from thinking the worst about himself and worrying about me. Later that evening I told David about the voice and how I thought he might think I was nuts. He didn't, it was all in my mind I guess.

The police came and left, my dad came and left, and I was finally alone. When everything settled down and the room was empty I heard that voice again. It was a male voice that said "Cynthia, why didn't you listen to me?" Huh? Who are you, I said? It's me pause.... God.

This is where I need to give you a little background into my life so you will understand where I was coming from before we go further with my story. I accepted Jesus in my heart when I was 8 years old or so in the church. After Mema passed away I began a fast descent away from God. I had begun to not care about what I did or who I hurt. Even my marriage was on a fast track out the door. Everything I did or touched was to be for my pleasure and nothing else really mattered.

My heart was cold and dead. So when this voice comes again I am scared to death.

"God, wait how can that be, my church told me you do not talk to people anymore?"

Oh, really He said. Not everything they tell you in the church is the truth. The Word is the Truth and you must read the Word and decide if the church you are going to is telling the Truth. I have never stopped talking to my people and I never will. I tried to stop you from going to the fair, but you would not listen, so I allowed Satan to run over you with that truck but not to kill you. If you don't turn your life around and change I will allow Satan to kill you next time.

This was a total shock to my brain in every way possible. What God allows Satan to hurt people if they are not following or listening to the Lord can speak to people out loud if He wants? Believe me, I had all kinds of questions after that. I suffered for two weeks in the hospital. Any time I moved that right hip it felt like someone crushing my side. It was a horrible experience. Along with this pain, I was having this horrendous experience. Every time I went to sleep I was at 5th and Dewey ready to cross the street. As I was crossing the street here comes a car and runs over me! The terror of being hit again was tremendous. It was slow motion and there was nothing I could do but go through this. After waking it would come again after falling asleep with exhaustion. It would be a train this time, same intersection, same pain same everything. Each time it was a different vehicle but I knew what was going on. I knew this heavenly being was making a point and I was going to get the point come hell or high water so to speak. Each time this train, plane, whatever hits me it is with such force it throws me 60-90 feet and tears up everything on my body. When all of a sudden I'm back at the intersection crossing the street when to my left comes a 14 wheeler.

'Oh Lord please not again. Yes, again!' He said. There was one more thing that I noticed and was unable to change anything in each episode. I was completely and utterly alone. No one or nothing was with me. I had chosen to leave the Lord so He was gone. This was worse than any death there is. I don't know how to explain it but we as people are very social. That is why people congregate with other people. We are not meant to be alone. And then two more weeks at home before I started to feel halfway normal. One of my doctors came and told me that the truck was right on top of my spleen and it doesn't take much pressure at all to make it burst and kill you on the spot.

He called it a miracle and I told him you don't know the half of it believe me. It took several months but I did get my life straightened out and back on track so to speak. This was a life-changing event that I will never forget and realized how very blessed I am to have had this experience. I was given a second chance at life and I refuse to tum away from God again.

SIX

The Test of a Lifetime

Cindy writes: This was one of those days that will forever be in our memories yet it was a typical day. Trenton our grandson was coming over after school and we always look forward to having him over. I was at the sink doing the dishes when I saw Tbone (our dog) trying to run across the lawn! Something was not right just by the way he looked and ran. I quickly went to the back door and yelled to David as Tbone was slowly coming to him. David, Tbone is sick or something he can barely walk or run! David had been busy in the barn working on something as he noticed our dog limping and collapsed on the ground. We both were with him in record time watching, wondering and in utter shock as he began to start foaming at the mouth and jerking. David grabbed the water hose and proceeded to run the hose down his throat. Water, vomit, and foam were all you could see and it looked bad. Tears came to David's eyes as he told me that Tbone had strychnine poisoning! I put it out back for the rats but I was sure Tbone couldn't get to it!

He is going to die, Cindy, he is going to die! David is now unable to stop crying at this point. This is his dog and companion and friend- I held Tbone's head and was praying with all my might under my breath and with an urgency that I knew was needed at this point. This is when everything kind of slowed down and became very clear. David go get me a chair I said. I need to have direct contact with this dog and I knew it. Okay, he said and off he went. He brought the chair and I told him to go and get Trenton now and we will be waiting when you get back. The look on his face was, are you sure you know what you're doing? Yes I do, everything will be all right just go. I KNEW I had to get David out of there because of his unbelief and doubt. He wanted to say goodbye to Tbone but I told him no, please go, Tbone will be fine, just go. He left with a broken heart and tears thinking he would never see his dog alive again. That is when it began in earnest. I prayed with everything I had. I told Tbone he would live and not die, he could drink any deadly thing and it would not hurt him. No weapon used against him would prosper. I quoted every scripture I could think of that had healing to it or life. His head was in my hands and I patted and rubbed his head watching his eyes looking straight at me with understanding. I will never forget the look he gave me as this was taking place. He knew what I was doing and he knew I could not stop or it would be over! Over and over I repeated out loud he would live and not die that God was healing him and he would run again on this land and be happy. I told Satan he could not have our dog that our dog belonged to us and we belonged to Jesus. I said Jesus over and over and over again. This was a battle and Tbone knew it and I knew it, and I was not giving up! My heart or Spirit knew if I put his head down and did not touch him and quit praying it would be over. This was a fight between life and death between good and evil between God and the devil, and I was not giving up! After what seemed to be a very long time, my heart knew he was going to be all right.

David drove up and came over to Tbone and me with a look of shock on his face. He's still alive, yes David and now you need to take him to the vet, and he will be fine. Off they went and I seemed to collapse with fatigue. Trenton was full of questions but I had no answers. This was above and beyond anything I had ever experienced. All I could do was praise the Lord for saving our dog!

The Vet was amazed for they said normally dogs don't make it this long after being poisoned like that. They gave him Vitamin K because of the bleeding that he had. Every tissue and every organ bleeds due to the poison" They kept him overnight and the next day I called the office and they said it was a miracle that he was alive but he seemed to be fine! We brought him home and he has been fine ever since" That was a test that day, did I believe what I had been studying in the Bible or was it just a book of stories to be read and not used?

Chapter

SEVEN

Silvia Will Never Forget

I met Silvia on a cruise ship headed to Cozumel, Mexico, and believe me it was a God kind meeting. Silvia and her roommate Mary where on a fun trip together. Silvia had gone to a vacation introduction package and received this free trip very similar to our trip. Silvia and Mary were our dinner table people that we sat with each night of the cruise.

I was sitting out on the Lido deck listening to the music when I saw Silvia and Mary walking up. I asked them to sit with me and we began to talk. How I got on the subject of miracles I will never know but I did. This is when she told me what happened to her. Silvia had been home that morning but a meeting was going to take place around 10:00AM. She had been told by God audibly at least 3 or more times not to go out that morning but she didn't listen.

Her last car payment was just made and everything was looking good. Her boss had told her several times don't miss this meeting. It was summertime and Silvia felt an obligation to make this engagement. After climbing into her car she was on the road. Who needs a seat belt anyway? Her son was in the car and had to be dropped off at the nursery. After dropping him off it was time to go. It didn't take long before she had fallen asleep. Silvia hit a police officer and he hit her on the passenger side and threw her into a spin. The rearview mirror hit her in the head and her head hit the windshield. Despite the damage, she remained conscious.

After getting his thoughts together the officer went and checked on Silvia. The police officer looked at Silvia and then looked at the car with utter amazement. Lady, I don't know how you did this but it looks like an angel or something big stopped you from going through the windshield! Her eyelashes had been ripped from her eyes yet her eyes were not hurt! God supernaturally put an angel in front of her to stop the force of her body from going further than the windshield. Yet at that moment in time, Silvia didn't have a clue to what had happened. She was more concerned about her car than her safety and the safety of the officer involved. An ambulance came and took her to the hospital. Later that evening when everything calmed down and she was all alone the Lord spoke to her again and said "You didn't listen to me." You would think that this would shock her into reality but it didn't. This did shake her up enough to start thinking differently. Thank goodness God doesn't give up on us when we are in denial which Silvia was at the time. As time went on and she had other God encounters and she finally started to listen and obey. As a matter of fact, this was the beginning of her many encounters with God watching over her and her family.

EIGHT

Garden of the Gods

It was around September 1968 and I was finally home from the hospital after being struck by a boat and partially paralyzed. I had spent the summer lying in bed watching TV waiting to find out where my life was going to go. For a 15 year old that can be an eternity. Thank God the paralysis from my chest to my feet was finally starting to get better. I could walk now with the aid of crutches and a lot of arm strength. It was good to be home. This one particular night will forever be in my memory and forever in my heart.

I fell asleep as usual but I started dreaming I was at home walking of course (without any crutches) it is an interesting note that in every dream, I have I am walking without the aid of anything when someone came to the back door knocking. It was Mr. France from next door. I opened the door and he told me "Cindy this is the strangest thing, you have a phone call at my house." Okay, I said with some hesitation. He said, "this phone that is at our house is in our back yard and it is not our phone!" I'll be right over and off I went. Mr. France was confused and, a little frightened. As I got to the front door I could see straight into the back porch and yard. Mr. Frances's back yard had always been plain and a huge rut all along the fence where his French poodle had run. It was normally plain and boring so to speak. But as I looked out this was not their normal back yard, it was beautiful! This backyard had a kind of mist look to it almost translucent with trees, flowers, and waterfalls. The strange thing about this yard was it seemed alive with life almost singing! Everything moved and swayed with their independence and happiness. This took me by surprise so I stopped at the back door in amazement. Mr. France was in front of me telling me look there is the phone I told you about. I looked down to see a phone that was sitting there with no cord to the phone or the wall. This must be a joke I thought but then again what is going on with this back yard? I grabbed up the handset and said in quick session hello, hello, hello, not thinking anyone could be on this phone. The whole time I am never taking my eyes off this wondrous lawn! An operator said may I speak to Cindy Allen, please? I could not believe it, this phone is for real but I could not get my eyes off of this beautiful back yard! Yes this is she, I said; when to my surprise another woman was on the line. Cindy this is your Mom how are you? No, it is not, I said how dare you to try to act like my Mom, my Mom is dead.

"Yes, I know" she said, ask me three questions only your Mother would know?

"Okay, fine lady, I will play your game, what is my father's full name?" "Lawrence Allen", she said. "Okay, you got that right, how about my name?"

"Cynthia Allen."

"Okay for sure you won't get this one, what is my Mothers full name?" "Mattie Estelle Scott Allen, Cindy it's me."

I was in utter shock and could not speak at that moment except to say "Momma?" "Yes Cindy it's me, I don't have a long time to speak to you so I need to tell you why I am calling." "Okay, what is going on?

The Heavenly Father has allowed me to call you to tell you that I love you and that you need to quit holding hatred in your heart towards me. She said sickness is what caused me to act with anger and hostility towards you. It was never your fault and I wanted to tell you how very sorry I was to treat you the way I did, but I always loved you. Well, you didn't act like it! Thoughts of her yelling, spanking, cursing were brought to my memory. Every single memory I had of my mother was bad, nothing in my mind was good. Yes, she said I know that is why I had to talk with you. Cindy, you cannot hold bitterness and hatred towards me and have a good relationship with the Heavenly Father. In fact, you cannot have anger towards anyone and still have a relationship with the Father! Wow, that was quite a surprise to me. Somehow I felt that after all those years I had a perfect right to be mad, bitter, and angry! This phone call was becoming a real revelation to me.

She knew what I was thinking and would answer accordingly. After what seemed like such a short time she told me, look in your baby book you will see how much I love you. What difference does a baby book make I thought I don't understand this. How can this make any difference?

I kept my eyes on this beautiful garden/backyard as we spoke, it was comforting. She told me that she needed to tell me one more thing and then she had to go. What about this backyard I said? She said what do you think it is? Heaven, I said? No it's not heaven it's Paradise. In fact it is a small portion of Paradise; you could not handle or understand Heaven. The Heavenly Father has allowed you to see a small part of Paradise. Paradise is one of the first places you go before entering Heaven. I had never heard the term Paradise, after talking to Mom, I found it in the Bible. Now Cindy, listen to me, you must talk to your Father and tell him not to do what he is thinking about doing or this could jeopardize our reunion in heaven. What? What are you talking about Mom?

What do you think I am saying she said?

"Suicide?"

"Yes, that is it."

"No way, Dad would never do anything like that."

"Yes, he would Cindy tell him about our conversation and he will change his mind. Now I have to go, so remember what I told you and I love you very much."

I immediately took my eyes off of the backyard and said" wait", but it was too late the phone disappeared in my hand and on the table. I looked up and the backyard was the same old backyard I had always known. It felt like the world had caved in on me and there was nothing, I could do to save it. For a few minutes, I stood where I was hoping that maybe the Paradise would come back and the phone would return but for some reason I knew it was gone forever. I slowly walked back through their house not wanting to speak to anyone. As I moved through the house every step felt like doom. The peace I had felt was gone. After being in Paradise, this world has nothing to give.

I don't remember opening any doors or closing any doors I just walked out of their house. As I walked up to my house as soon as my foot hit the back step I woke up!

My mind was in a spin the dream was clear, I remembered every bit of it. I yelled for Dad but I heard nothing. Fear gripped me thinking Daddy had maybe already killed himself. Grabbing my wheelchair I loaded myself on it and went straight for the bedroom. He wasn't there.

I looked all through the house, nothing. The last place was the back door. There he was. Dad was sitting on the porch smoking his cigarette. He helped me come down the ramp when I brought up the subject of my dream. He listened as I told him everything in the dream. When I got to the part about what Mom said about Dad. He asked me what she said? I told him you are not going to believe what she told me about you. What did she say? Mom said you were thinking about killing yourself! It was dark outside but I could see that he had been crying. All he could say was, how could you have known? How could you have known unless your Mom told you? I lost it, with anger I said Dad how could you have even thought such a stupid thing? You are all I have in this world who would have taken care of me if I didn't have you?

"All I could think is that if I was dead you would be better off without me!"

"What? Are you kidding? Nothing on this Earth could be farther from the truth!"

He grabbed me, hugged me and kept saying, you must have talked to your Mom; you must have talked to your Mom. There on the porch that night, Daddy promised he would never think about doing that again. Later the next day I found the Baby book and it was filled with her thoughts about how much she loved me and was so glad I was her child. There is hardly a day that goes by that I don't remember that dream. Dreams come and go and I can never remember them but this dream never goes away. That was 43 years ago. I found out in the Word of God later that you cannot hold anger, bittiness, etc. towards someone even for a day if you want to be forgiven from the Father. Dad lived till he was 71 and died in the hospital from complications. If he had lived he would have had to go to a nursing home and he never would have been happy there. That might have been a dream but I know that on that day I talked to Mom on a heavenly phone. And I got a glimpse of a small bit of Paradise. God is so good.

Chapter

NINE

Fear and Trembling

It began to snow that night and the next morning my family and I woke to the beautiful scenery of snow everywhere. The school was official out due to the snow. Kyle was around 10 years old when this happened. He had a friend named Roger who lived in another town a few miles down the road. Before I knew it Kyle was asking me if he could go sledding down Moore hill with Roger. No! I said. Something didn't seem right. I couldn't explain it but I knew deep within my spirit something was wrong but I couldn't put my finger on it. At 1:00 PM Kyle began a well-calculated plan to bug me till I would finally give in and let him go. It seemed to last for hours but maybe it wasn't that long. I finally let my resistance down and said go I am warning you, to be very careful. Before I knew it he was running out the door with his coat, gloves, and hat.

As soon as his body was out the door a dread came over my spirit that knew I had made the wrong choice. I can't explain how or why I knew I knew why I knew or what it was but I knew that it could be bad or very bad, I just didn't know. That is when I begged God to forgive me and spare Kyle. Please I pray, do not let anything happen to him.

For at least an hour I prayed continually asking God to protect Kyle and to watch over him and forgive me for not being a better parent. It was one of the longest hours I have ever spent knowing deep within me Kyle was in real danger and there was nothing I could do to help him other than pray.

Moore Hill was an actual road. It was in a small town so when it snowed the kids and grownups would use this road as a sledding place. Only experienced people would go down this hill. It was dangerous. Meanwhile, he got to Moore Hill and he came down the hill on the sled and for some reason, he spun around and fell off the sled with his head facing up the hill. As he was looking up he noticed another kid headed straight for him with one of the old fashioned metal sleds. Before the sled hit him Kyle passed out! The boy ran over Kyle's whole body but his right arm was lying out and hit with enough force to break it and the collar bone. If Kyle had not passed out when he did the kid would have run over Kyle's head and done major, major damage. Kyle remembers looking down on his body seeing a couple of dogs grabbing his stocking cap and one grabbing his gloves.

The next thing he knew he came too and next to him where the two dogs with his stocking cap and his gloves. He got his belongings and went to Roger's in a lot of pain. Roger's dad drove him home and by the time he got there both of us knew Kyle was hurt.

Later that night after we got home from the hospital is when I heard the whole story about his wreck. Kyle had never passed out before this time nor has he ever again. I believe the minute I started praying God was lining up angels ready to help a young boy from being seriously hurt or possibly killed" I thanked God for sparing Kyle and forgiving me for not listening.

TEN

Bridgette's Fight for Life

This is from my dear friend Bridgette who had written me a letter back on Jan. 7, 1992. Bridgette is with the Lord now but this experience she had was a real miracle. Let me tell you in her words what happened. I was working at this store, having been sent there specifically to witness to a young man (21) who had left the Lord. I had just started developing a relationship with him, which I can assure you were anything but friendly. I knew he was married, had met his wife once and she was very pregnant. One evening I was as usual at my kitchen table reading the Bible, this time it was IISam12. The story of Bathsheba. As I read the verse "the child is dead" God's gentle voice clearly said to me "the baby is dying". I was immediately confused as I didn't know any babies. I wracked my brain going through a mental inventory of friends; church family, everyone I could think of and then I remembered that the young man, I'll call him Bob. His wife was pregnant though I had no idea when she was due. The word burdened to pray isn't proper in this case. I was filled with this Power to pray. I do not have the gift of praying in the Spirit but in every other sense of the term that is what I experienced that night. I truly comprehend Jesus sweating blood as He prayed. I felt wracked and torn as my spirit was praying so hard for these unknown babies. I had to retreat to my bed and lie down. As every ounce of my being was involved in prayer. The words were not eloquent I worried that all I could do was repeat the same prayer over and over again. I felt such Power being given to me should require a flow of sacred words yet the simplest pleas were all that came forth. When I retreated to my bed, having no strength to even sit up, I found myself standing in the dark space of our universe. This has always brought to my mind when Paul had his revelations on the isle of Patmos is how it is for me. I have no idea if this vision overtook my mind completely, of if I was there. My spirit I mean, I'm sure my body remained in bed though I was unaware of it. There were opposing forces of angels and Lucifer angels, they looked alike to me, dressed in white but they fought as if there was a broad path between them. One group on one side the other group lined up on the other side, fiercely fighting. I believe that the space between them was my prayers were to go through and Lucifer angels were there to prevent my prayers from reaching the Lord. Now there is nothing in the Bible that even hints at that to my knowledge, but that is how I interpreted it though I may be wrong in my understanding. I just stood aside in the vast dark universe watching and praying. The praying went on for 3 to 5 hours I can't remember which and though I truly was frantic because all was saying a thousand times over was 'save the baby, save the baby" I didn't dare stop. Then suddenly I was released and I found myself lying in bed, quite at peace. Exhausted, I slept. The next day I went to work as usual, and as I opened the door to enter the store and employee came rushing up to me and asked if I'd heard Bob's baby was born last night and she had almost died! Can you imagine how I felt? It was like a rosebud blossoming in my heart! I know I glowed. What had happened was at a crucial moment in the baby's birth the cord was discovered to be around her neck, so an emergency caesarian was done. The baby was born around 11:00 PM which is when I was released from the prayer. But what I've always found interesting is that the Lord called me to prayer hours before anyone was aware the baby was in danger. I presume I had a vision. It certainly should convince anyone of the importance and power of intercessory prayer.

Chapter

ELEVEN

The Hospital Inside the Hospital

Here is another story from a friend I had met online years ago and have lost complete contact with so I have changed her name and some other key places. She had given me her story so 1 could put it in my book. Here goes: You asked me to tell you about my near death experience. I had graduated from college and had received my diploma etc. on a Friday evening then went home and tried to do some housework and found that 1 was weak and a little out of breath. Saturday, I did grocery shopping and had to sit down twice in the store (this had never happened to me before) and I had a hard time lugging the groceries into the house and putting them away I just kept telling myself that I was exhausted. I went to the hospital Saturday afternoon to visit a relative who was there for minor surgery and I noticed how weak and tired I felt walking down the hall. I went home and lay down on the couch too tired to make dinner. My son came home and said that I looked tired but did I stop, NO. I went to the beach with Peter, my son. It was early evening and the beach was very quiet but I was completely out of breath and had to rest twice before making it down to the water's edge. I found that I couldn't swim – too tired. I sat on the beach and needed Peter to help me get to the car. I do not remember that Saturday night and all that I remember of Sunday (it was Father's Day) was that I felt exhausted not really sick a little bit feverish and terribly thirsty but nothing remarkable. Monday morning my sons had to wake me, I was in a great deal of pain which I attributed to my gall bladder, it was that type of pain. I asked them to call my boss for me (I was starting a brand new job) and explain that I would be in later that I was going to call my family doctor and get some antibiotics. When the boys left for school, the pain intensified. I called the doctor and got an appointment for 11:00 it was now about 9. The nurse asked if I had a fever so after I hung up, I thought I'd take my temperature. It was 106 and the pain was getting worse and I was developing a wheeze. It hurt to breathe. I called the doctor back and said that I needed to come in earlier. I told the nurse about my fever and she told me to call 911. l called them and collapsed on my porch waiting for them to arrive. I only bothered to mention all of-this mundane stuff to try to show you how sneaky this virus is. It hits fast and heavy and if I had not called 911 and gotten to the hospital when I did I would not have survived. I remember the first hour or so of the emergency room then nothing more until late that evening when I was put on a ventilator and had chest tubes inserted. I heard this one doctor telling another that I would not make it through the night. My lung had collapsed and could not be re-inflated. I was in terrible pain and the morphine really did not work that well. I remember hearing a doctor telling my sons youth minister that I had about a ten per cent chance of making it through the night and that he should probably start preparing my kids. I have no relatives other than my children so it really was hard on them and I do not know how we all would have made it without the church. I went in to a coma at this point and didn't wake up for 11 weeks or 82 days.

I remember being in a lot of pain and floating around the ICU unit. I saw the doctors there at the nurses' desk; they were discussing me and a plan of action. They did not know then that it was pneumonia and that there was a silver dollar size hole in my lung that had been eaten away by the bacterial infection. My blood pressure had dropped real low and they all started running around my bed as 1 watched them from above. I could see myself in the bed but I remember thinking that was not the real me. I heard a swoosh sound and I was back in bed and in even worse pain. I was upset that the doctors didn't really talk to me but around me or about me. The pain was getting unbearable and for the first time I was frightened. I was alone in the ICU cubicle and in terrible pain with tubes everywhere and terrible sounding machines. Three men came in.

I had never seen them before but just seeing they put me at ease. They told me that I was very sick and that I could go with them away from the pain. They gave me a decision. I said that I wanted to go with them but they said that I had to think the decision over. I started worrying about my kids. I really felt panicked and told the men that I had to stay with the kids. They said that I would be okay but that I would be sick for a while and that they would stay with me. I told them how frightened I was and they said to "trust". I then felt myself transported to this other hospital it was very pretty and the bed that I was in was on this big porch. There were hospital beds to my left and I understood that those people were dying. I could not see their faces. There were people to my far right and I understood that these people were getting well and there I was in the middle. There were other beds there and other people but I didn't communicate with them. I can still feel the feelings that I had at that time and I can still remember the dream state that I was in while I felt I was in this other "hospital". I went through 4 lung surgeries had two teeth knocked out from the ventilator tube I had a track tube put in and I remember none of it. I can still recall the events from the dream state though. They were as real as anything else that has ever happened to me. The men were there in the background and occasionally told me not to be afraid.

I cannot really expect anyone to believe me but I have spoken to others who have gone through similar things. I had to spend a long time at a rehab hospital after I regained consciousness and talked to other people there with similar experiences. I do not know how to explain it but ever since this experience, I have felt light, I do not worry as much as I used too, I enjoy more now and it really has had a profound effect on my outlook on life. I truly believe in God and in a life hereafter and I would never again fear death. I felt safe and cared for those 11 weeks and have kept that feeling with me ever since. This is called Necrotizing fasciitis. Or also called "flesh-eating disease."

Chapter

TWELVE

God's Miracle House

This is a friend of mine who had gone thru a terrible divorce after many years of verbal as well as spiritual abuse. She had 2 children and the Lord had told her that she was moving to Austin, Texas. She didn't even know Austin existed at that time. Her home in Louisiana didn't even belong to her until the next to the last court battle. She obeys the Lord and puts the house on the market. Almost immediately she gets a buyer for her home. This is exciting and a new adventure for her and her little family. Heading down to Austin to look for a home she gets the highest credit rating there is and is approved for home loan without any job! Instead of buying a home she decides to have one built. As this home is being built with no income coming in her home in Louisiana had something come up with the couple who were buying it, and now their credit is no good. They are no longer eligible to buy a home. This is now the month of June and her new home is almost ready to move into. In the meantime the bank wants her to do a walkthrough on the new home. The inspector goes through the new home and they found the house to be defective. My friend goes through the house and is appalled at everything that is wrong with it.

The Bank wants to close on the new home in the month of July but cannot because of defects. The builders said they fixed all the problems but would not let the Real Estate Agent walkthrough the home. This is now a huge mess, her home she lives in is now empty with no buyer. Her new home is defective and not fit to move into. This is the month of August and the bank is threatening her to move into this defective home and sign the contract. She is officially homeless. She is continually praying. The Lord tells her to let go of the house she is buying. I can't she said, "look at all that money I put down on that house, I will lose those funds" Again He said, "you need to let it go". You need to trust me daughter. This was hard for her as she had 2 children to raise. They were living in a hotel at the time. Again she would go into the other room and cry out to God to change this situation. Finally she told the Lord, "I will let go of the house." Within the same day and almost the same hour she had released the home she got a call. It was the builder and they said because she didn't close on the home they were dropping the contract. Eight Thousand dollars lost. Her new home is gone along with the money she put down. But on the same day as this awful news came in she receives word that a Christian couple looked at her home in Louisiana and liked it. They put an offer on it and she accepted the offer. But as homes are concerned this couple was going to have to come up with $20,000.00. My friend was concerned so many things had gone wrong and the time was short. It was no problem for this couple they came up with the money within record time. As God was speaking to my friend after she gave up the house He told her something incredible. He said Daughter, "you are going to be moving into your new home within 24 hours." This really made her think because she has no job, no husband, 2 kids and the animals. Plus she lost $8,000.00. My friend has huge faith so she believes the Lord and goes on. Her Real Estate friend had 10 homes that they were trying to get rid of. She goes to see each and every one of them. On the 9th home it was brand new. Some people had tried to buy it when the mortgage fell through. It was a larger home than the one they were buying plus the appliances were all free which she didn't have at the other new home. They dropped the house down $25,000.00 and she said you need to do better than that and she walked off to the next house. As she was looking at the 10th home, the builder from the 9th home called her and said if she would buy the home they would drop the price down to another $20,000.00 plus pay the closing cost and all she had to do was pay $500.00 down if they approve the loan. He then said you could be in your new home in no time! She said yes of course closed on the house She was in her new home within 24 hours just as the Lord had said. She also had all their furniture that was in storage that was going to be lost in 3 days. God is so good He got that furniture right before her time was up! Nothing is impossible with God.

Chapter

THIRTEEN

A Glimpse of Heaven

My friend had a spirit of fear when all of this was going on. With her health issues of Cancer, I can understand why. So she had a dream that she was in this building it was very dark and she was lying on this thing that looked like a doctor's bed. These demons came down and she said very mildly -you flee in Jesus name. Nothing happened. So again she said in the name of Jesus flee. Again nothing happened. On the third time she spoke with authority and COMMANDED THEM TO LEAVE IN JESUS NAME, be gone I mean it, she said. About this time a big huge light comes down thru the roof and sucked up all the demons. She travels out of the building and she sees a narrow highway. Which for instance is a scripture on the narrow highway and how we have a choice to either take the narrow highway and be in Gods will or on the broad highway which represents the world. Matthew 7:13-14. The NIV States: Enter through the narrow gate. For wide is the gate and broad is the road that leads to destruction, and many enter through it. 14 But small is the gate and narrow the road that leads to life and only a few find it. So she starts running down this narrow highway and she ends up in heaven. Her voice changes here:

and she said, oh my, just a glimpse of heaven makes you want to go there. People were smiling at her with flawless skin. The colors in heaven are beautiful; they have colors there that we know nothing of. Then apparently Jesus is standing in front of her. She said people here say when Jesus has a robe on its purple and purple stands for authority and royalty. But when she saw him he stood before her in a white robe with a blue scarf like piece of material hanging around his neck. Karen was no longer in heaven. She kept trying She kept trying to get into heaven and he said no my child. She remembers his eyes, and his love and his gentleness. But despite that she still kept trying to get into heaven even after He said, no my child. But as she awoke she said she was ticked because she still was not in heaven.

FOURTEEN

Healing of Breast Cancer

K aren had 3 weeks to live and it was in her lymph nodes and they scraped it off of her right rib. The Doctor than told her she was going to die. It just kept getting worse. She was on a guinea pig protocol chemo regimen which had not been approved by the FDA they were studying her. It got to the point she could not keep anything down water or Ensure. Her husband Mark called the hospital and they put her on a feeding tube a few times to keep her strength and energy up. She was 88 pounds at 6'1/2", tall. Karen was actually getting her spirit ready to pass on at this point. But as she did, her family kept coming to her mind. Her elderly Mother, her 2 girls and their families, her son and his family. She called the Cancer Treatment Center telling them of her dilemma of not being able to eat. And at 3:30am she tells them she is not going to make it to the next appointment because she will be dead. They asked her if she could self-medicate herself till they get an appointment set up. She has not eaten in 8 days at this point. She asked her can you get a hold of a joint without getting caught for her appetite. This of course was when marijuana was not legal. The lady went on to say until we have a meeting at 6:30am and legalize you?

Karen said yes I think I can. She was able to get that joint and smoke it. She woke up the next day and felt joy. Karen said she leaped out of bed in the morning and felt she was healed. She had no nausea, no weakness, or dizziness. She had hunger which hadn't happened since the cancer had progressed. After putting on her makeup and putting on her wig she walked up the street to a convince store and got something to eat. Proceeding to the phone she called chemo therapy and said "I quit."

"But wait just a minute you haven't done radiation yet, Karen said

"I don't have too I am healed" and hung up the phone. This is when she told me "when you know you are healed you are healed."

As I questioned her about the marijuana joint and asked her if the joint healed her or not and she said no. The only thing it did was give her an appetite. She said the marijuana is natural and it is made by God also.

I really wanted her to tell me if she thought the joint healed her or not. And again she said no it did not. It was God who healed her and Him alone.

Chapter

FIFTEEN

A Vision You Don't Want

This is one of the strangest things that I have ever happen to me. I am changing some of the details to this story because I don't want to hurt anybody by telling their story. It was a long time ago back when I was a young Mother and wife. It was a Friday afternoon and was headed to the bank with my husband's check. I got to a certain part of the road and all of a sudden I saw myself in an accident. This accident was horrendous. I was a passenger in my car when all of a sudden something hit us and my chest hit the dash and my head went thru the windshield. All of this is going on as I am driving down the road. For some reason I knew it wasn't going to be me but it was someone else. I was floored. Where did that come from? Am I losing my mind? What is going on? I kept having that vision over and over and over. I got his check and went to the bank. I knew because of other strange things that have happened to me to not talk about this kind of stuff around friends or family. So I finally got home. David came home and said you are very quiet today what's going on? Not much I said. It was horrible. I wanted to tell him yet I was afraid. Afraid maybe this was a friend, maybe us. I didn't know for sure. By Sunday, I couldn't keep it a secret any more so I told him. He listened and was understanding but he didn't know what to do either, it was a crazy experience. Hopefully it will all go away and never return. Monday evening David came into the house and was yelling for me before he barely got in the door! You are not going to believe this honey?

"Oh yeah what?" Remember that vision you had? Well someone from his office had gone to a movie with his wife and on their way there a car or truck hit them and his wife hit her chest against t the dash and her head went thru the windshield! She was dead.

"No way" I said.

"Yes, it happened that night."

"I, I....... cannot believe this!!!"

We discussed it for a while but I felt sick at my stomach. I had done nothing. I didn't pray for this person. That's why it had happened. I was to pray. Why didn't you tell me Lord? Why the guessing game? I am a single person not even a very religious person. To this day I regret that decision I made that day. I kept wondering why, but never prayed. Was I the reason she passed away? Was I the reason they had the wreck? Not every story has that good ending or happy ending, but if this story helps just one person to pray for others than I have done my deed.

Chapter

SIXTEEN

What Does this Mean?

David and I had been dating a short time. We met at school; he was the cute guy in my new math class. Being on crutches due to an accident was no fun at all but I was going to make the best of it as possible. So because of the crutches I had a hard time carrying my books. I asked David to carry my books, he didn't fight it. Our school was large it was a combination of 7th 8th 9th grade on the right of the school and the 10th 11th 12th on the left side. I was in 11th grade at the time. We started to date pretty quickly after the books were being carried. He lived at home with his Mom and his younger brother, and two sisters. They lived on an extremely busy road that looked off of the river towards the west. One night I went to sleep and had the craziest dream. I saw David getting off of work and climbing in his car. He had a 57 Chevy at that time. As he was driving I was following close behind. Not in his car but from behind and above. I was actually flying, it felt natural. But it seemed like someone, somebody wanted me to follow him, so I did. Everything was going along fine till he came up to a certain overpass. This was not an overpass that was close to his house or close to mine. I really didn't understand why he was here at this overpass at all but here we are. He is coming up to this overpass and I see him hit the guardrail on the right nothing major happens not even a scraped fender. He hit it again but this time when he hits it the car flies off the overpass crashing below some 60 feet down! I immediately wake up.

I am in utter terror at this point so I call him up no answer. This seemed so real, what are the chances that he was laying in the street below, hurt or even dead? I was so scared! No I can't think like this. I just can't. You see I had some dreams that actually came true so this was one of my worst fears. Was that normal to have your dreams come true, I don't know? But it was normal for me. I liked him, I liked him a lot and I didn't want to lose him to some stupid overpass. The phone is now ringing. It's David thank God..... That is when I asked him about the overpass. Yes he had driven over that overpass but nothing happened. Were you on the right side by the guardrail? Yes, he was. Everything I saw was exactly what had happened except for the wreck. Was I the reason he didn't wreck that night? Was I seeing the future? What was this? I don't know the answer much less the question. I'm just so happy he didn't wreck that night or any night after that.

Chapter

SEVENTEEN

Excited Why Not?

As I was making my rounds at the hospital I came into a young man's room in his late teens. He was so excited to see me which I thought was quite unusual, being I didn't even know him. He went on to tell me how he had met Jesus during a routine surgery. He got a glimpse of a heavenly place and was overly thrilled. The colors were out of this world, more beautiful there than here and colors we don't even know about. This city was huge and everyone was so happy. No death there, not even a blade of grass. Then he met Jesus, oh his eyes, you can never mistake those eyes. He had these holes in both of his hands. But it was time for my friend to go home. Yes, he said I am so excited. That's when he got the shock of his life. He wakes up in the hospital. What's going on? Why am I here? I thought he meant up there. That is when he tells everyone from the janitor to the Doctor. There was only one problem, no one believed him. He told everyone he came in contact with about his encounter with Jesus and heaven. It got to be very frustrating to him. This very spiritual experience was being shattered by well-meaning friends and family. An experience like this is so wonderful and so heavenly many people choose to not tell anyone just because of that reason. It is an experience of a lifetime. He gets excited again and tells someone else. They proceed to tell him he was dreaming, the medication did it, his surgery put him in a trance like state, etc. etc. etc. As I listened to him explain yet one more time, of all that is in his heart, I take several deep long breaths.

"I believe you", and "I know you saw Jesus. You do, he said? "Yes I do." My heart is heavy and yet it is light also. If only I could tell him everything I know on the subject. This has been a life-long interest of mine. If there were any books on the subject, I'm pretty sure I have it in my personal library. I know of 4 different times I have come very close to dying myself. I guess that is why I am writing this book. I want people to know we are not alone we are here for a reason. With all of that said, I wanted to comfort him and tell him everything is going to be all right. But I couldn't because now that he has seen it, he knows it is true. He no longer needs faith for this experience; he has seen Jesus and the city. Ok young man may I make a suggestion to you? Yes, of course. I think he was so excited to hear that someone actually believed him he would have said yes to almost anything. It's a very tricky kind of experience that not everyone needs to hear about. Tell someone that you trust with deeply personal things. Write it down so you remember the details because as we age some of those items in the story itself fade away. I wished him well and had to move on to the next patient.

Chapter

EIGHTEEN

The Lords Protection

How did this happen? But yet Elizabeth knew, in her heart and her spirit. She was 9 months pregnant, entering the hospital. This was going to be a wonderful experience, so she thought.

Elizabeth's Mom had just arrived, she was all smiles and happiness was everywhere. Beth as people liked to call her was not so happy. Her Mom and Dad had divorced at the age of 12 and she had been raped at the age of 14. She was told that this rape had caused damage to her female organs so more than likely she would or could not have any children. After finding out that she was pregnant at the age of 17 she dropped out of High school. Times were different back in the 70's. Nobody got pregnant it was taboo so to speak, and being unmarried was the talk of the town! The Father of this baby was involved but his family hated her and everything about her. So it is no wonder she was extremely depressed. Somewhere in the middle of all of this she had a Nervous Breakdown. How can anyone love her she thought? Her Dad was not here to protect her and her Mom had been too busy with life outside of the home. Now it was time to deliver. Mom was in the waiting room and Dan (Dad) was with her. It was not a surprise that, Dan's Mom and Dad were not in the hospital, they had chosen to be of no support for either one of them. It was not the everyday normal kind of birth. Beth was now in full labor with her blood pressure off the chart being wheeled to the Operating Room. It was Toxemia; she was now in all kinds of trouble. The doctor worked feverously along with any nurse who was willing to help. She was given drugs to sedate, and Beth was out like a light. When to her surprise she was above her body looking down! How is this possible, she thought? Am I going crazy? In a frantic frenzy he started cutting on her to bring the baby out. Above her body Beth, was starting to feel fear, as she knew this might be the last time she would see this child. Beth was raised in a traditional Christian home, not the every weekend church home, but close enough. As they pulled Conrad out, Beth felt a rush of love. This was her boy and he was beautiful. How can she get back? Doctor I'm up here you need to do something, help me please!

The Doctor who was giving the drugs started yelling, we're losing her, we're losing her. The baby was quickly rushed out of the room and the atmosphere changed instantly. Beth was relieved that finally someone was taking care of this situation. As they worked to try and get her body back Beth felt sadness. Nothing will ever be the same. Her son would be raised by another Mother and Beth would lose all those years with her small family. Every thought and every emotion seemed to flood her mind at this point. Mad one second, fear the next, sadness, as well as joy. Every thought held in her mind at this point. She could not control any of these thoughts and they we're playing havoc in her mind. Out of the blue everything went blank. Now in a hospital room, her mind started to come back, she recalled it all! Was that a dream she thought? Am I as crazy as I think? What really happened? A nurse walked in about that time and asked her if she needed anything? Well as a matter of fact can I speak with the Doctor please, she said? Yes of course, he will be right in. Awhile later her Doctor came in with his normal jovial face. After speaking of non-important things, Beth gets right to the point. Doctor did you know that I died on the operating table? Well I huh, pause....As a matter of fact, yes you did come very close to dying. I know differently and I was actually floating above my body when you took the baby out. It didn't really matter at this point if the doctor believed or didn't believe Beth knew that something very out of this world happened to her and nothing would ever be the same. Within a few short weeks she knew that she had grown spiritually. Someday each of us will have to take that journey but in the meantime we can learn about it by hearing Elizabeth's story.